CONTENTS

I WANT TO BE A JUGGLER

You'll have to practice hard and be very patient, but the effort will be worth it! Don't try to learn too much at one time. Take it slowly and before you know it, you'll be juggling without even thinking about it. At this stage you can start planning a show for your friends.

When you can juggle with three balls, you're ready for a show!

You can practice indoors and outdoors.

Make your own juggling balls using rice and balloons.

Plan well ahead for the big show – send out invitations, make posters, and rehearse your acts.

Juggle with your feet as well as with your hands! Find out what to do when a ball goes astray!

Juggling is a great way to make friends. Teaching other people how to juggle will help your patience and your own juggling.

GETTING READY

One great thing about juggling is that you really don't need much to get you started!

The right size to fit in your hands

These are ones you can make yourself.

What to juggle
When you are an expert, you will be able to juggle just about anything. But it is a good idea to begin with something soft and unbreakable.

Why juggle?
Juggling is an activity that nearly anyone can be good at. Juggling can help you feel calm and relaxed. It is a great way to get rid of tension.

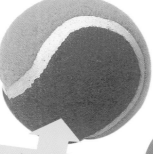

Wait until you're an expert for this one!

Not too bouncy!

Beanbags are easy to catch.

Eggs are probably not the best things to juggle!

Beanbags are easy to juggle because you can catch them by their corners. If you'd like to make your own juggling balls, look on page 16.

Perhaps this wasn't the best place to practice?

TIPS

★ Keep your beanbags or balls with you everywhere you go – you never know when you will have a spare moment to practice.
★ Don't rush through the pages. Take it slowly, and only learn a new trick when you are confident.
★ Juggling has more to do with rhythm and pattern than thinking.

I could have told him that!

Where to juggle

Choose somewhere where you will have plenty of space. Make sure there is nothing breakable nearby – when you begin, your throws may not be very accurate! After a while, you will be able to juggle anywhere because you will have learned control.

Practice makes perfect

Learning to juggle needs lots of patience. Don't get upset when you drop a ball – even the greatest jugglers make mistakes. So, now that you know what you are in for, it's time to get started!

LET'S GO!

It may not look like juggling, but practicing with one ball is the best way to start. Even when you are an expert, it will help you get your rhythm.

Looking relaxed
Stand in front of a mirror and practice your juggling position.

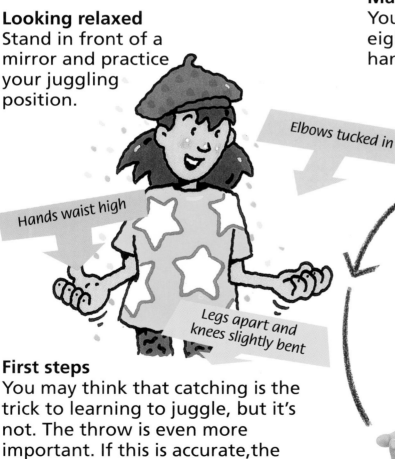

Hands waist high

Elbows tucked in

Legs apart and knees slightly bent

First steps
You may think that catching is the trick to learning to juggle, but it's not. The throw is even more important. If this is accurate, the catch will take care of itself.

Scoop the ball
Everything about juggling should feel easy and relaxed. This includes the way you throw the balls from hand to hand. Practice a gentle toss, rather than a jerky throw. It may help if you think about it as a scooping motion. Try not to look at your hands when you are juggling.

Making a pattern
Your throws should make a figure eight. The scooping throws from each hand should go across your chest.

This is called a cascade pattern.

How high?

Aim for a point level with the top of your head. The ball should travel in a gentle arc. You should not have to stretch forward or twist your body.

Try not to think too hard about what your hands are supposed to be doing.

Save your legs!

A good way to avoid stretching or twisting is to stand facing a bed. This will also make it easier to pick up the balls when you drop them.

I think I'm getting the hang of this. I'll keep going until I can do ten throws and catches.

Which hand?

Most people have a leading hand that seems to be more obedient than the other. But if you are going to be a successful juggler you will have to make sure that both hands work equally as well. This will probably mean practicing hard to make your weaker hand strong.

I'm not coming out until he gets better at this!

TIPS

★ Throw from your fingertips (they control the direction) and catch in the palms of your hands.
★ Have you cheated yet? Put that second ball away! Set yourself targets at each stage to stop yourself from racing ahead too fast.

... THEN TRY TWO

By now you should feel very confident throwing and catching. It's time to be daring and introduce a second ball. Don't panic!

1 Using exactly the same inward scoop throw as before, throw the first ball up in an arc toward the other hand.

2 When the first ball reaches the top of its arc and starts to drop into the other hand, throw the second ball up. It should pass just underneath the first ball. Keep going!

3 When the second ball reaches the top of its arc and starts to drop into the other hand, throw the first ball back toward the other hand. Keep going. It may help to count out loud: 1, 2, 1, 2, 1, 2 . . .

TIPS

★ Practice starting with different hands. Your weaker hand will soon become strong.

★ Make sure you throw both balls to the same height. You may be tempted to pass the second ball across to the other hand! This is a *bad* habit.

Safe landing!

If you have problems when you start juggling two balls, don't even try to catch them. Instead, let each ball fall to the floor. Look where the balls land. If your throws are good, they should land close to your feet – not miles away. Practice doing this until the balls always land in the same place. Then try juggling again.

Exactly the right position. If you can make them land like this, you should have no problems at all.

READY FOR THREE?

Are you sure? Now is your big moment. Take a deep breath and pick up the third ball. Stay calm and read through the instructions first.

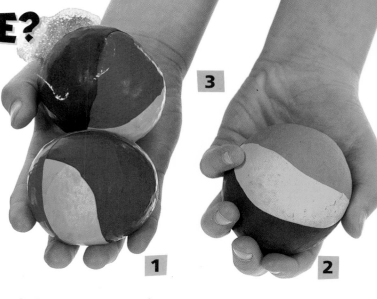

Patterns in the air

The easiest juggling pattern to learn is the cascade, where the three balls appear to cross in midair. All jugglers use this pattern in their acts. It is great to watch and not too difficult to do.

1 Try to remember everything that you have learned so far. Hold two balls (or beanbags) in your best hand and one in the other — see picture above.

2 Throw ball number **1** up in a gentle arc toward the other hand.

3 When the first ball reaches the top of its arc, throw ball number **2** from your other hand up in a similar arc. It passes under the first one. Don't panic, you're nearly there!

5 When the third ball reaches the top of its arc throw ball number **1** back up in an arc underneath it. Repeat the pattern from the beginning, and don't forget the figure eight.

4 When the second ball reaches the top of its arc, throw ball number **3** from your stronger hand up in an arc. It passes underneath the second ball.

TIPS

★ Don't rush your second throw. Wait until the first ball has reached its peak. It may help to count out loud as you throw each ball. Then you will hear the rhythm as well as feel it.
★ If things aren't going smoothly yet, don't worry. Turn the page to find some tricky tips.

TRICKS OF THE TRADE

Here are some helpful hints for making your juggling smooth. But one of the most important things to remember is *practice makes perfect!*

Don't wobble

It is important that you juggle in the same plane. This means that your juggling balls should not be in front of each other, or to the side. Look at the picture below to see what a side view of a perfect juggler looks like.

Remember, don't rush. Make sure you are an expert with two balls before you go on to three.

You can do it!

Try teaching someone else to juggle. This will help you see the problems from a different angle. It will also give you even more practice in being patient.

Perfect juggler

Perfect plane

It may help to imagine you are juggling while standing in front of a picture frame. When the balls are in the air they should reach the top two corners of the frame. If you are constantly moving and stretching to reach for balls, you will be outside the frame. Are you still having problems? Go back to one ball again. That usually works miracles!

Aim for the imaginary corners and you'll soon get the idea.

Move around

To improve your confidence, try juggling while walking around or when you are talking to a friend. You might be surprised how many new friends you make!

Left or right

If you find that your weaker hand is letting you down, give it some extra training. Everything you can do with your best hand you should learn to do with your other. Use your weak hand to throw a ball against a wall. Don't stand too far away. Do the same exercise facing the wall and also standing sideways.

BALLOON FUN

If you have tired yourself out juggling, now's the time to sit down and make your own juggling balls. Perhaps you could make a set for your friend as a present, too.

What you need

You can make juggling balls out of plastic sandwich bags, a little rice, and small balloons. Split peas or any other kind of dried beans may be used instead of rice. Tape the plastic bags completely closed.

1 Blow up a balloon and then let the air out. This will make it stretchy and easier to work with.

2 Put a handful of rice or split peas into a plastic bag. Don't fill it too full or your juggling ball will be rock hard!

3 Fold over the top of the plastic bag and secure it with tape.

7 Add one or two more balloons in the same way. If you use different colors you will be able to make a pattern.

4 Cut the neck off the balloon about a quarter of the way down.

5 Pull the balloon over the plastic bag. If there is any surplus neck, snip it off.

Let's go! Time to learn some more juggling patterns.

6 Stretch and cut the neck off another balloon. Pull it over the plastic bag in the opposite direction to the first balloon.

SOMETHING NEW

Here are some new juggling patterns to learn. They use skills that you have already learned.

Reverse cascade
So far, you have juggled using underhand scooping throws. For the reverse cascade, throw overhand. The figure eight pattern stays the same.

Release the ball at shoulder height.

Try one ball to start with. Toss it up using an outward scoop.

Catch the ball at waist level.

Now add a second ball. With the reverse cascade, each new ball goes *over* the previous one instead of underneath it. Practice with two and move up to three.

This takes three balls. Use the first two balls to keep a cascade pattern going. Toss the third ball over the top of these balls from hand to hand. Balls one and two doing the cascade are the tennis net and ball three is the tennis ball. Get it? This is a good pattern to use when you come to put on a show, because it looks much harder than it is!

Juggler's tennis

You don't need a tennis racket for this juggling pattern. Just a lot of practice! Juggler's tennis is a mixture of cascade and reverse cascade, so make sure you can do both before you try it.

Don't make the outward throws too wide or you won't be able to catch the ball.

Outward scoop throw for reverse cascade

Inward scoop throw for cascade

STOPS AND STARTS

By now you probably feel as if you have been juggling forever! It's time to add a bit of showmanship to your act. Let's see how you can vary the pace a bit and cover up your mistakes – if you ever make any!

▼▼▼▼▼▼▼▼

Kick it up!
If one of your balls drops on the floor, don't panic. Simply trap it between your heels and pretend you know exactly what you are doing.

If I keep smiling, nobody will guess that anything is wrong!

Aim to get the recovered ball back neatly into the juggling pattern

Practice with one ball first

Keeping the ball wedged between your heels, kick your legs up to the side and release the ball so that it flies over one shoulder and back into the juggling pattern. If you do this well, everybody in the audience will think it is a fancy part of the act.

Pause for effect

When you have been juggling fast and furiously for a few minutes it is a good idea to slow down for a while.

Practice catches on your forearm, back of neck, foot, back of hand, or wherever it feels comfortable.

Gentle foot roll

Here's another easy way out of trouble. Roll your dropped ball or beanbag casually onto your toe using the other foot. Kick it back up into the juggling pattern.

Try slowing things down by catching one of your beanbags on a different part of your body. This will surprise your audience and give you a second to get your breath back.

Not too hard or the ball will hit the ceiling

The top of a straw hat provides a great landing pad for a beanbag.

Pretend you have lost your beanbag for a second before zipping it back into the juggling pattern.

COLUMNS

It's nearly time for the big show! The more tricks you know, the more exciting your act will be. So practice hard to master this new pattern.

Straight up and down

With columns, the balls do not cross each other in the air. They move up and down in their own plane. The only slightly tricky part is learning to juggle with one hand.

Make sure you practice with both hands, not just your best one!

Easier than it looks!

Juggle two balls in columns using your best hand. Move the other hand around at the same time, not necessarily in any set pattern.

Move this hand in time with the blue ball.

Now take a ball in your other hand. Each time you throw *one* of the balls in your best hand, move the third ball in your other hand up and down parallel to it. This will create an amazing optical illusion!

Don't throw the third ball, just move it up and down.

The real thing

Now it's time to *really* juggle in columns! Start with two balls in your best hand and one in the other. Throw the first ball from your best hand straight up through the center of your body.

When it peaks, throw the other two straight up on either side of it. When the two balls peak, throw the single ball up again.

TIPS

★ Remember the tip about juggling in the same plane. These will help when you are juggling in columns. Try to keep the columns separate.
★ Throw the balls in each column to the same height.

It's getting easier and easier every day!

DOWN AND UP

Not all juggling happens up in the air. Why not try juggling down for a change? Or if you are feeling really hot, you could try juggling under your leg.

When you are feeling really confident juggling down, you could work out a routine combining juggling up and down.

Bouncing back
You can use any of the patterns you have already learned to juggle down. As before, it's best to start with one ball, then you can add a second, then as many more as you think you can manage.

Use extra-bouncy balls.

When the ball hits the floor, it is at its peak.

Make sure the floor is not bumpy.

This is one way to keep in shape!

Lift your knee up as high as you can.

Before you throw the ball under your leg, throw the one before extra high to give yourself more time.

It's best to wear fitted pants for this so that they don't get in the way.

Knees up!
Start your juggling pattern by raising your knee and throwing the first ball under it. Each time you throw a ball with your best hand, lift the same knee up and throw the next ball in the pattern under it. Put your foot back on the ground and continue the pattern.

Don't try this with your best sweater!

Boing, boing . . .
This is definitely an upward trick. Start a cascade pattern. Throw one ball extra high in the air. Holding a ball in each of your hands, grab two corners of your sweater. Let the high ball land in the dip in your sweater. Pull the corners tight and the ball will shoot back in the air, and with a bit of luck you can get back to the pattern.

TASTES GOOD!

Even jugglers feel hungry from time to time. But you don't have to stop practicing to have a quick snack. Juggling with food is a good act to include in a show.

An apple a day
Apples and oranges are good for juggling because they don't get squashed if you drop them.

I'll have to be careful not to take a bite out of a juggling ball!

Before you get too carried away, practice with one apple and two juggling balls or beanbags. Juggle a normal cascade pattern.

Up and over
When the apple arrives in your best hand, throw the next ball in the pattern extra high. This will give you time to bring the apple up to your mouth for a quick bite. Lower your hand and continue the pattern.

Don't be tempted to take a second bite, there isn't time!

Keep on munching
After a bit of practice you can try this trick with three apples. If you don't like apples, try pears.

Avoid anything that needs to be peeled!

NEARLY THERE!

You've been practicing and practicing and now it's time to show your friends just how good you are. Here are a few things to think about before the big day arrives.

Arranging a space

You will need an area to stage your show and your audience will need room to sit or stand where they all have a good view. Find a good place and arrange some chairs or cushions for your friends to sit on. If the weather is good, you can put on your show outside!

Ask your guests to reply so you know how many people are coming.

For an indoor show, you could make a stage from cardboard and colored paper.

Invitations

Once you have decided on a place, date, and time, send out invitations to your friends. Make your own from colored paper and send them out at least a week before the big day.

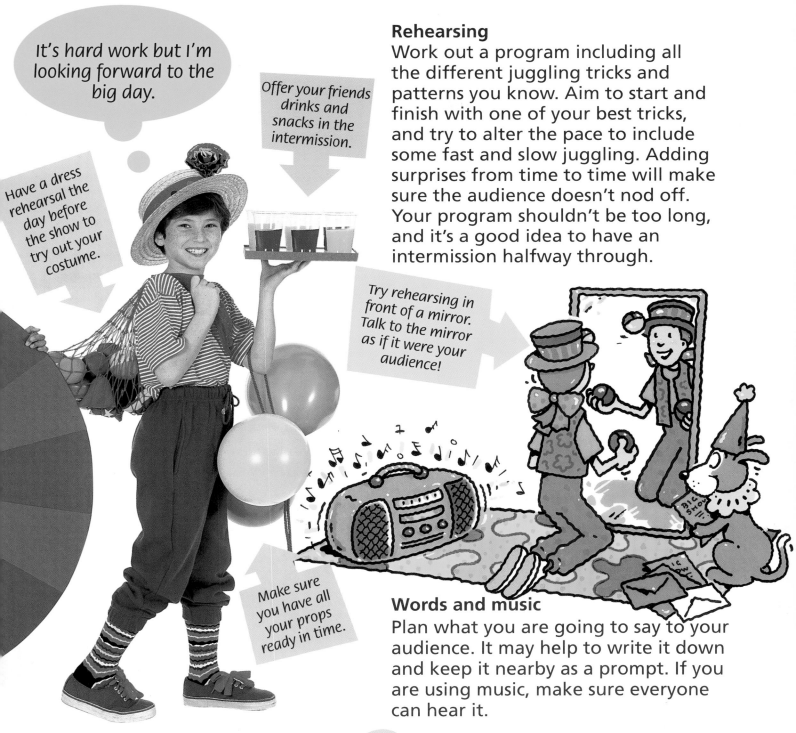

It's hard work but I'm looking forward to the big day.

Offer your friends drinks and snacks in the intermission.

Have a dress rehearsal the day before the show to try out your costume.

Rehearsing

Work out a program including all the different juggling tricks and patterns you know. Aim to start and finish with one of your best tricks, and try to alter the pace to include some fast and slow juggling. Adding surprises from time to time will make sure the audience doesn't nod off. Your program shouldn't be too long, and it's a good idea to have an intermission halfway through.

Try rehearsing in front of a mirror. Talk to the mirror as if it were your audience!

Make sure you have all your props ready in time.

Words and music

Plan what you are going to say to your audience. It may help to write it down and keep it nearby as a prompt. If you are using music, make sure everyone can hear it.

SHOW TIME

The big day has arrived and it's time for the show! The audience is sitting down and there's no time to feel nervous. Make sure everyone is comfortable. Take a deep bow and start juggling!

Ladies and gentlemen, please give a big welcome to Tom, the greatest juggler in the world!

Present the performer loudly and confidently. Make the audience feel excited.

Ask a friend to help you with the show. He or she can share the work that goes into preparing for the big day and can appear onstage as your assistant. It's good experience for someone who wants to put on his or her own show. The assistant's first job is to introduce you to the audience.

BEFORE YOU GO ONSTAGE GET RID OF ANY LAST MINUTE NERVES BY HAVING A GOOD STRETCH AND SHAKE TO LOOSEN UP!

★

HAVE FUN WITH YOUR COSTUME. SEARCH IN JUNK SHOPS AND GARAGE SALES FOR CLOTHES THAT YOU CAN ADAPT.

★

LOOK FOR SILLY HATS TO DECORATE WITH PAPER FLOWERS OR POM-POMS.

Assisting a performer is an important job. The assistant should be ready to help out if any disaster happens!

INDEX

It's goodbye from me and the rest of the gang!

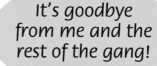